25 Days of Dece

Jesus' *Unexpected* Family Tree

Kristin Kjorlaug Dobrowolski & Lorena Albright López

Created in Allentown, PA
and Ponferrada (León), Spain

ISBN: 978-1-7329532-0-8

Published by Gray Ink Media

Artwork by Kristin Kjorlaug I kristinkjorlaug.com

All Scripture verses
are quoted from the ESV Bible

Dear Reader,

December is finally here! Homes all around the globe are starting to plan and decorate for Jesus' birthday celebration. It's going to taste, smell, and look so good by the end of the month—all this preparation for one birthday.

Although the message of a birthday is simple, it's important. Birthday's are a chance to say to a dear created human, "I'm so glad you were born and are here with us!" And so in the same way, Christmas day is our chance to say to Jesus, "We are so glad that You were born and came to be with us on earth!"

Jesus' Unexpected Family Tree is another visual reminder in your home of God's great story. As you prepare for the biggest birthday celebration of the year, you could print the ornament PDF at kristinkjorlaug.com or purchase the Jesus's Unexpected Family Tree Ornament Coloring Book to be used as daily reminders of what we are celebrating on the 25th. These ornaments can be hung on your tree each day of December. You may just enjoy coloring them or creating your own ornaments. Thank you for celebrating with us this year!

Messy and included,

Kristin Kjorlaug Dobrowolski

&

Lorena Albright López

Introduction

This is the story of a family, and the portrait of this family looks a lot like a messy painting labeled, "Jesus' Family Tree." You may be thinking, "My family tree is messy, too!" But Jesus' family tree isn't a mess... is it?

What was Jesus' earthly family like? We know he had a family tree because every human does—parents, grandparents, siblings, uncles, and cousins all in crazy lines going all the way back to where every family begins, in a beautiful and perfect garden. So wouldn't you expect God to paint lots of beauties, or heroes, or religious people in a family meant for Jesus?

Yes, but what we notice instead are some pretty disappointing, ugly, and broken people all over this family portrait. "They don't seem to fit and they're making a big mess of the painting," we might say. But, surprisingly, God looks at the mess and sees the kind of people He loves to include.

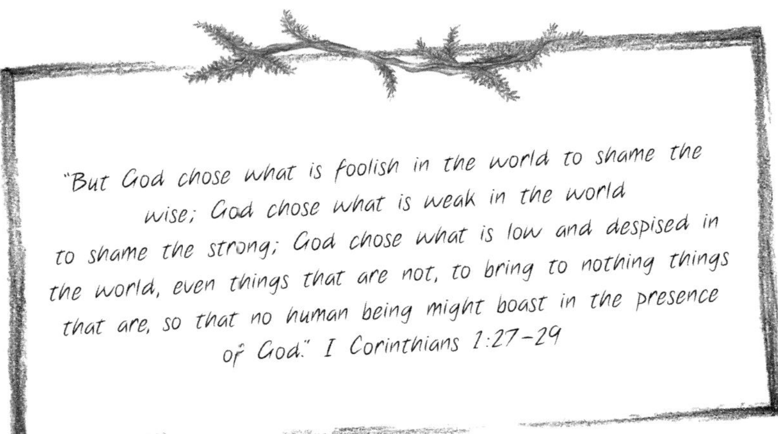

Creator of Family

December 1st

Today is the first day of December, a month we all anticipate! But the story of December actually begins with God—where all things begin. The idea of family was in God's mind before He even created the world. He wanted to share the special relationship that the Trinity had been enjoying for so long. And to do so, He created humans to walk and talk with Him in the most marvelous garden ever imagined. God designed this masterpiece of relationship by putting humans into families. They would be close to each other and close to God. The example was perfect. Family was a beautiful idea.

"Then God said, 'Let us make man in our image, after our likeness...'" Genesis 1:26

To earthly families: "Therefore a man shall leave his father and his mother and hold fast to his wife, and they shall become one flesh." Genesis 2:24

For more on this story of Creation: Genesis 1-2

God

Human

December 2nd

Can you imagine being the first human on earth? How amazing it would have been to walk and talk with God in the garden! Adam was fantastic and looked so much like the One who made him, but so different from all the other creatures around him. Like a son is a picture of his father, Adam resembled God in this first family portrait, and they loved being together.

God had created this place just for humans and He had a special task for Adam: to be a father to a family and to take care of God's creation. Humans were to explore Earth, eventually designing all kinds of tools and buildings, and exploring science and cultures. All this was given so that families could flourish and humans could show what God is like in a million different ways. But it was Adam's first days on this earth that would forever shape the relationship people experienced with God.

"And God blessed them. And God said to them, 'Be fruitful and multiply and fill the earth and subdue it, and have dominion over the fish of the sea and over the birds of the heavens and over every living thing that moves on the earth.'" Genesis 1:28

"The LORD God took the man and put him in the garden of Eden to work it and keep it." Genesis 2:15

For more on this story of Adam: Genesis 1:26-2:25

Adam

Broken

December 3rd

God shaped Eve from Adam's rib. Although she was strikingly different than the man, she too, looked so much like God. Eve enjoyed a perfect relationship with both God and her new husband, Adam. But something caught her eye and she looked away from God. She and her husband followed the snake past branches heavy with fruit to eat from the one tree God told them not to. This was a boundary God knew was good, but Adam and Eve didn't believe him. Their disobedience broke the perfect relationship they had with their Creator. No more walks with God. No more garden. Shame and death were their shadow.

But God didn't let their story end here. He whispered hope to the broken woman and man, "From your children will come One who will crush the snake." God promised that somehow, someday, there would be a baby from the family of Adam and Eve who would crush the snake they had foolishly trusted. He would rescue them from this brokenness and restore their garden-relationship with God. "Who will this Rescuer be and when will he come?" they wondered as they walked away from the garden.

"And they heard the sound of the Lord God walking in the garden in the cool of the day, and the man and his wife hid themselves from the presence of the Lord God among the trees of the garden." Genesis 3:8

Speaking to the snake, God said: "I will put enmity between you and the woman, and between your offspring and her offspring; he shall bruise your head, and you shall bruise his heel." Genesis 3:15

For more on this story of Eve: Genesis 2:18-3:24

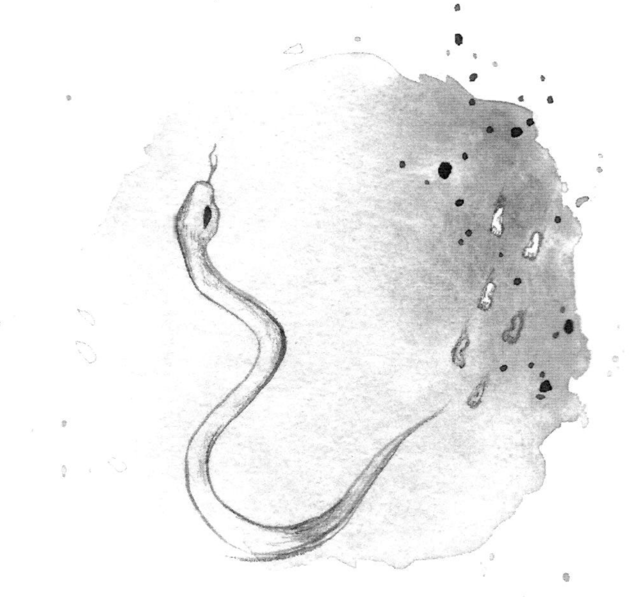

Eve

Chosen

December 4th

Adam and Eve marveled at this miniature human squirming inside Eve's belly. Maybe this child was the one God was talking about? But, oh the agony she felt in her body as the tender new baby was pushed into the harsh world outside the garden. "Is this the pain I will feel with each new baby?" Eve wondered. Yes, it would be, but it would feel nothing like the heart-wrenching stab of this first child growing up and killing his brother. All hope of these children fixing this tragically broken world was shattered. One son was dead and the other a life-taker. This was awful! Far from the garden, pain, endless work, and death followed them everywhere.

But God wasn't surprised by any of this, and knew what life would be like without Him. He already had an unexpected plan to bring his dear humans close to Him again. Adam and Eve had a third son, Seth. Although he was not the Rescuer they had hoped for, this child would be the one God chose to begin the growth of a family. The family tree of Jesus had a stem.

"...She bore a son and called his name Seth, for she said, 'God has appointed for me another offspring instead of Abel, for Cain killed him.'" Genesis 4:25

For more on this story of Seth: Genesis 4:1-5:8

Seth

Lonely

December 5th

Adam and Eve's family did grow to great numbers on the earth, but these people were still living on their own, away from God and His good boundaries, as their first parents had. There was no one that looked like a rescuer to them, and few even remembered what God had said about him. Noah was a little strange to them because he talked with God. Even stranger, Noah was building something huge just because God asked him to. Oh, the laughter that must have swirled around Noah and his sons as they worked on this massive structure.

How lonely it must have felt for Noah's family in these years, and even more so when they were floating on the silent waters covering the earth. What now? How could God possibly rescue them with just eight lonely people left on earth?

"By faith Noah, being warned by God concerning events as yet unseen, in reverent fear constructed an ark for the saving of his household." Hebrews 11:7

"Because they formerly did not obey, when God's patience waited in the days of Noah, while the ark was being prepared, in which a few, that is, eight persons, were brought safely through water." I Peter 3:20

For more on this story of Noah: Genesis 6-9:19

Noah

Trusting

December 6th

Abraham, whose name means "Father of the multitude," was still not a father and getting quite old. But God picked Abraham's little family of two and whispered a promise to him, "From you will come a baby, and this child will be a blessing to all the people of the earth. Can you count the stars above you? Your family will be more than the stars you see!"

Unbelievable? At first glance, yes! But Abraham stepped forward towards this promise and the God who spoke it. At times he did not understand what direction to go, and made some big messes. But unsure step by unsure step, Abraham found that God could be trusted. God was painting a big family and Abraham was the next in line.

"God said, "Sarah your wife shall bear you a son, and you shall call his name Isaac. I will establish my covenant with him as an everlasting covenant for his offspring after him."" Genesis 17:19

"Therefore from one man, and him as good as dead, were born descendants as many as the stars of heaven." Hebrews 11:12

For more on this story of Abraham: Genesis 17, Romans 4, Hebrews 11:8-12

Abraham

Childless

December 7th

Sarah had followed her husband, Abraham, for so long that living in tents was all she knew. But through these many years, her tent had been empty and quiet, with no child to hold or teach. Now, her husband was 99 years old.

An empty ache in her old body twisted painfully when she overheard men nearby tell her husband that they were about to have a baby. "Isn't it a little too late for that?" she laughed. The idea of being a mother at this age was impossible to her. But within the year, God placed a child beside her in her tent—just as He had promised! This new baby was an unexpected addition to the growing family of Jesus.

"The Lord said to Abraham, 'Why did Sarah laugh and say, 'Shall I indeed bear a child, now that I am old?' Is anything too hard for the Lord? At the appointed time I will return to you, about this time next year, and Sarah shall have a son." Genesis 18:13–14

"The Lord visited Sarah as he had said, and the Lord did to Sarah as he had promised. And Sarah conceived and bore Abraham a son in his old age at the time of which God had spoken to him." Genesis 21:1–2

For more on this story of Sarah: Genesis 18:1-15, 21:1-7, Romans 4:18-25, Hebrews 11:11-12

Sarah

Rescued

December 8th

If Isaac, Abraham's special promised son, died, how would God grow Abraham and Sarah's family to number more than the stars? He was just a boy, too young to have his own children! Wasn't Isaac the only hope for continuing God's chosen family for Jesus? Actually, no. God is the only hope for this family.

On the mountain, God spared Isaac's life at the very last second—a rescue that would resemble His own unexpected plan for Jesus. A ram caught in a bush would die instead of Isaac. This one, who should have died, would now live many years, having children of his own. He was rescued by God and included in Jesus' family tree.

"By faith Abraham, when he was tested, offered up Isaac, and he who had received the promises was in the act of offering up his only son, of whom it was said, 'Through Isaac shall your offspring be named.' He considered that God was able even to raise him from the dead, from which, figuratively speaking, he did receive him back." Hebrews 11:17–19

For more on this story of Isaac: Genesis 22:1-19

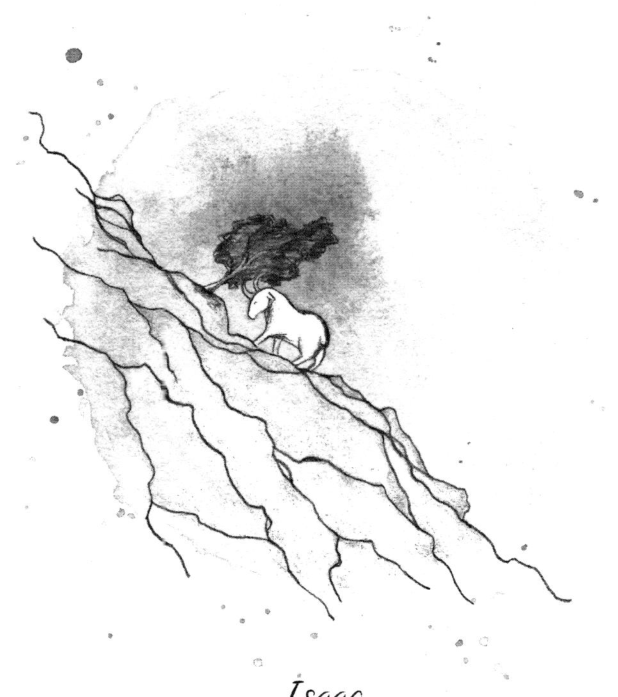

Isaac

Far

December 9th

Rebekah hugged and kissed her mom, dad, brothers, and sisters goodbye. She sensed that this would be the last time she would ever see them. It was clear to her, however, that she should go with Abraham's servant and marry this very special son he had told them about. Abraham's servant had been searching, sent on a long quest to find this specific bride for Isaac. The only clue he had was that this lady would give water to his camels, showing unexpected kindness to a stranger.

God had known exactly where she was and how to find her. "I will go," Rebekah said willingly. In Rebekah's story, God reached far, far away to include her in the family of Jesus. But is anything really too far for God?

"And they called Rebekah and said to her, 'Will you go with this man?' She said, 'I will go.'" Genesis 24:58

"Then Rebekah and her young women arose and rode on the camels and followed the man. Thus the servant took Rebekah and went his way." Genesis 24:61

For more on this story of Rebekah: Genesis 24

Rebekah

Deceiving

December 10th

"Rebekah had twins!" they told Isaac, "and the second baby grabbed the heel of the first!" This heel-grabber grew up deceiving his family and grabbing for the blessing that traditionally and rightfully belonged to the older brother. He eventually got what he wanted with his sly tricks. Surprisingly, God took this grasping liar from the womb and put him in Jesus' earthly family tree.

God later changed this deceiver's name to Israel, which means, "one who wrestles with God." His family would be called Israel from then on. Sadly and true to their name, they would wrestle with God for many years to come, not trusting the One who would never deceive them.

Isaac to Jacob: "But he said, 'Your brother came deceitfully, and he has taken away your blessing.' Genesis 27:35

God to Jacob: "Your name shall no longer be called Jacob, but Israel, for you have striven with God and with men." Genesis 32:28

For more on this story of Jacob: Genesis 25:19-34, 27:1-45, 32:9-28

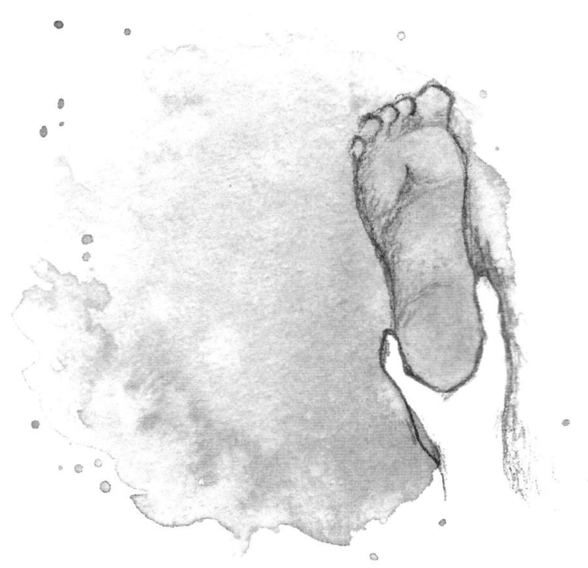

Jacob

Unloved

December 11th

Heart-ripping rejection rose in Leah's heart. It was a sick lie whispered over and over to her by the people who were supposed to love her—her family. "Nobody wants you—not your father or your husband Jacob, not even your sister. You know Jacob prefers your beautiful sister over you! You don't belong in this family!" Feeling ugly and unloved, Leah's heart was crushed.

Who could mend such a deep wound? God saw Leah and loved her. He knew all about broken hearts and the humans who break them. It was his delight to paint her into Jesus' family tree as a picture of God's love for the despised and rejected.

"When the LORD saw that Leah was hated, he opened her womb..."
Genesis 29:31

For more on this story of Leah: Genesis 29:15-30

Leah

Fierce

December 12th

"This time I will praise the Lord," Leah said to her fourth baby boy. "Praise" was the meaning of Judah's name. But as Judah grew up, he did not praise God. In fact, his heart raged with hatred and jealousy. So much so that he and his brothers almost killed Joseph, their own brother, but decided to sell him instead. What a surprise when Joseph's slavery was the exact tool God used to rescue the brothers who hated him.

One of these brothers, Judah, would be next in Jesus' family tree. God accurately described Judah as a fierce lion, and He promised that from the children of this man a ruling King would come to rescue them and lead humans rightly. But this ruler wouldn't be as they expected. God had a different plan for this family portrait, and Judah couldn't do anything to destroy the picture.

Joseph to his brothers, including Judah: "As for you, you meant evil against me, but God meant it for good, to bring it about that many people should be kept alive, as they are today." Genesis 50:20

"Judah is a lion's cub; from the prey, my son, you have gone up. He stooped down; he crouched as a lion and as a lioness; who dares rouse him? The scepter shall not depart from Judah, nor the ruler's staff from between his feet." Genesis 49:9–10

For more on this story of Judah: Genesis 29:31-35, Genesis 37, Genesis 45, 47, 50:15-21

Judah

Unwanted

December 13th

"She must die!" Judah cried coldly. He did not know that this was the woman who would keep his family alive. Everything seemed to be against Tamar. Twice she had married Judah's sons, but was widowed soon after. Now Judah wanted her gone. Why? Well, she was pregnant and had no husband. "Who is the father of this child?" he yelled.

Judah raged against her, ready to rip her out of his family, until he saw his own name seal and staff from her hands. He was the father of the child in her womb. And so we find that God wanted Tamar. He quieted her accuser and placed the unwanted woman and baby in Jesus' family picture.

About Tamar: "As she was being brought out, she sent word to her father-in-law, 'By the man to whom these belong, I am pregnant.' And she said, 'Please identify whose these are, the signet and the cord and the staff.' Then Judah identified them and said, 'She is more righteous than I...'"
Genesis 38:25-26

For more on this story of Tamar: Genesis 38:6-30

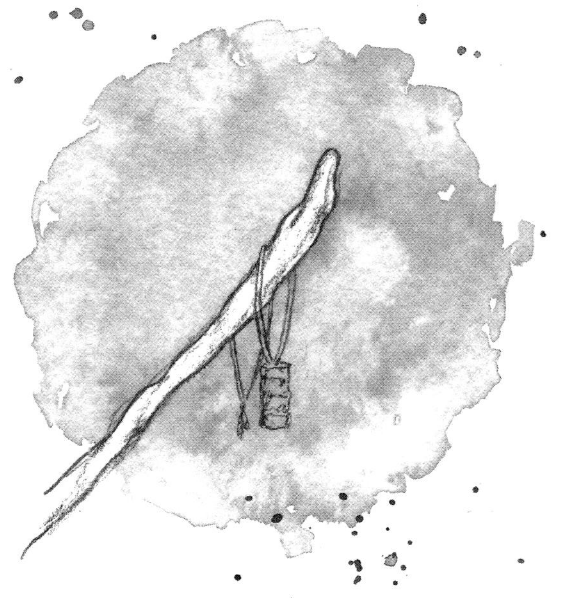

Tamar

Destroyed

December 14th

Rahab did not belong to this family called Israel, but she had certainly heard about them and their God. Stories of what happened to Egypt and the desert kings were whispered nervously around her, and now their armies were marching toward her city, Jericho. "We're going to be destroyed!" she thought in dread, knowing that Jericho did not listen to this God or obey anything he said to do. She hadn't either, but fear melted her heart.

The big walls Jericho trusted would come crumbling down on top of them. But one house remained with a red cord fluttering in its window. Rahab was alive in that house. The cord she hung signaled whom she trusted. God graciously pulled her from the rubble where she should have died and put her in the arms of a new family, Israel. This one who was almost destroyed is also painted into Jesus' family tree.

Rahab to the spies: "I know that the Lord has given you the land, and that the fear of you has fallen upon us, and that all the inhabitants of the land melt away before you." Joshua 2:9

For more on this story of Rahab: Joshua 2, 6, Hebrews 11:31

Rahab

Foreign

December 15th

Ruth felt all eyes watch her as she twisted and beat the sweet grain with her bleeding hands. It was obvious how far from home she was and that she didn't belong with these people of Israel. She smelled the precious grain that would be a small meal that night and thanked God for the owner of the field, Boaz. Her mother-in-law, Naomi, was right. "God truly does care for the poor, the widows, and foreigners!"

Unknown to her, God was about to invite her to eat at the family table of Israel, instead of collecting the leftovers. Ruth would be an unexpected addition to this family, welcomed by God. The way God included her in Jesus' family tree would declare to all humans that God chooses foreigners too.

Ruth to Boaz: "Why have I found favor in your eyes, that you should take notice of me, since I am a foreigner?"
Ruth 2:10

For more on this story of Ruth: Ruth 1-2

Ruth

Busy

December 16th

Boaz was a busy man, hard work consumed every ray of sunlight. But he was like most in Israel's family—just trying to survive. Boaz had wheat and barley fields and many workers to manage during harvest. So much to do. Not enough time in a day. No time to stop. Yet Boaz did.

Maybe he stopped because his mother, Rahab, had been a foreigner. But Boaz laid aside his work to secure a home and a family for Ruth, the foreigner on the edge of his field. "You see by this sandal," Boaz said, "that I have bought back all that belongs to Naomi, and will take Ruth as my wife." Taking the sandal meant he would keep his promise of redemption. Ruth may have added to his busy workload, but God added Boaz to this increasingly busy painting of Jesus' family.

Boaz speaking to Ruth: "Do not fear. I will do for you all that you ask, for all my fellow townsmen know that you are a worthy woman. And now it is true that I am a redeemer..."
Ruth 3:11-12

For more on this story of Boaz: Ruth 3-4

Boaz

Remnant

December 17th

Little is written about this man, Jesse. He was the grandson of Boaz and Ruth. We know that he lived in a time when Israel was failing, struggling without God. They did not trust the boundaries God had given them and were suffering the consequences. Far away from the garden, God was painting us a picture of Jesus' family tree when He described Jesse as a stump. A stump is a remnant. It's all that is left of a beautiful, once thriving tree—now sick, almost dead. But a tiny stem of hope would come from this stump, a son from Jesse. God would use this small branch to keep the broken family of Jesus alive. Although it would not look like a flourishing tree, it would survive.

"There shall come forth a shoot from the stump of Jesse, and a branch from his roots shall bear fruit." Isaiah 11:1

For more on this story of Jesse: Isaiah 11:1-10

Jesse

Insignificant

December 18th

They were on a quest for a king. Israel had a good idea of what they wanted: a handsome, tall, and confident king. "This towering Saul must be the one," they thought, but God was not interested in looks. He searches the heart. So, God sent his prophet Samuel on a much different quest. He sent him to the family of Jesse. Proudly, Jesse lined up his oldest and strongest sons for Samuel to look at. "No, not any of them," Samuel said. "Do you have any more sons?" Well, there was still the youngest boy, David, but he was out in the field with the sheep.

In this insignificant shepherd boy, God found a king to rule the family of Israel. Young David was the beginning of a royal line of kings that would both decorate and damage the family tree of Jesus.

"He chose David his servant and took him from the sheepfolds; from following the nursing ewes he brought him to shepherd Jacob his people, Israel his inheritance. With upright heart he shepherded them and guided them with his skillful hand."
Psalm 78:70-72

For more on this story of David: I Samuel 16:1-13

David

Disgraced

December 19th

Bathsheba was beautiful and King David noticed. This lovely lady became a queen in David's palace, because David took her through cover-up and scandal. She was pregnant with King David's child while being married to another man. Her husband was then killed, and her child would die soon after being born. Everything she had been living previously was quickly erased.

A woman broken, stolen, disgraced, and hurting, Bathsheba faded in the presence of David's other queens. But of all these beautiful queens, she was given the honor of mothering the heir to King David's throne. And then God surprises us again by also including this disgraced woman in Jesus' family, but should it really be such a surprise?

"When the wife of Uriah heard that Uriah her husband was dead, she lamented over her husband. And when the mourning was over, David sent and brought her to his house, and she became his wife and bore him a son. But the thing that David had done displeased the Lord."
2 Samuel 11:26-27

For more on this story of Bathsheba: 2 Samuel 11, 12:1-23

Bathsheba

Distracted

December 20th

With wisdom greater than any man of his time, Solomon searched. With riches more than any known king, Solomon searched. In every place that the sun touched and deep into the darkness, Solomon searched. Where was joy in this life under the sun? Wisdom, love, architecture, money, work, feasts—was it found in these? The mystery of these beautiful things and his many lovely wives distracted Solomon from the real joy he searched for. Sadly we watch as the wisest king of Israel foolishly worships the idols of his many wives, losing most of his kingdom. "How could he not know?" we think. But Solomon's heart, like ours, looked away from God.

By including this king in Jesus' family tree, God gave us a picture of every human heart—distractedly worshipping everything else. Solomon in all his wisdom could not see the future of the family he was in—the family of the One who would restore joy to these wandering hearts!

Solomon speaking: "I have seen everything that is done under the sun, and behold, all is vanity and a striving after wind." Ecclesiastes 1:14

"For when Solomon was old his wives turned away his heart after other gods, and his heart was not wholly true to the Lord his God, as was the heart of David his father." I Kings 11:4

For more on this story of Solomon: The Book of Ecclesiastes, 1 Kings 11:1-13

Solomon

Captured

December 21st

King Manasseh would most likely be remembered for rejecting every one of God's good boundaries during his reign. He also made sure to do the opposite of everything his father did as king. Listen to how God's prophets described him: "King Manasseh has led God's people into more idol worship than the wicked nations around them!" Then we hear God tell about the end of Manasseh's reign as king. "I will wipe out my people as one wipes out a dish and turns it upside down." And God chose this king to be in Jesus' family tree? The one he seemed to be finished with? The one shackled in bronze, being led away into captivity with his people? Yes, it's true. We don't expect God to use those who were against Him, but he did.

Someone beautiful would come from this seemingly useless family. Isaiah, the prophet of God, called him, "Immanuel". God had an unexpected plan to rescue broken people from their captivity.

"Therefore thus says the Lord, the God of Israel: `Behold, I am bringing upon Jerusalem and Judah such disaster that the ears of everyone who hears of it will tingle... and I will wipe Jerusalem as one wipes a dish, wiping it and turning it upside down.'" 2 Kings 21:12-13

The prophet Hosea to the nation of Israel: "Come, let us return to the Lord; for he has torn us, that he may heal us; he has struck us down and he will bind us up." Hosea 6:1

For more on this story of Manasseh: 2 Chronicles 33:1-20, 2 Kings 21:1-18, Isaiah 7:14

Manasseh

Repentant

December 22nd

Manasseh's grandchild was King Josiah. This child would take the throne at the age of eight when his father was killed. The family he was born into barely thought about God. Instead, they were talking to idols, trusting them instead of God, their Creator. As a very young ruler, Josiah was trying to destroy at least some of these idols. It was a valiant but impossible task. Jesus' family was so far from God, and had even forgotten that He had boundaries for them! Wherever they had been written down was now lost, unread, somewhere in the unused temple. When the scrolls were found and the words inside hit Josiah's ears, he fell to the floor in repentance. "We have not obeyed these words!"

How far they had strayed from God! Were they too distant for God to reach? Too far to be brought close again? Never! Haven't we seen how deep and far and wide God has searched for this family? But repentance was necessary to restore this brokenness, a picture God gave us by including Josiah.

"When the king heard the words of the Book of the Law, he tore his clothes...'Great is the wrath of the Lord that is kindled against us, because our fathers have not obeyed the words of this book, to do according to all that is written concerning us.'" 2 Kings 22:11,13

The prophet Hosea to the nation of Israel: "Come, let us return to the Lord; for he has torn us, that he may heal us; he has struck us down and he will bind us up." Hosea 6:1

For more on this story of Josiah: 2 Kings 22

Josiah

Humble

December 23rd

Four hundred long years had passed since they had heard from God. He was silent for so long that the promises he had made were fading from their memory. Had he given up on this family tree? Should they still hope in a Rescuer? Would God really send this Immanuel?

Then, finally, the silence broke! He spoke to this messy, shattered, waiting family. He didn't shout His plan to all of them, but whispered the good news to a few village people. Mary, a very young woman, sat dazed, wondering at the strange thing God's angel had just said. A baby from God inside her belly? Immanuel! How wonderful, and how terrifying! "Me?" Would anyone really believe her? "I am willing, Lord." Mary said humbly.

Once again, God finds the lowest and paints them tenderly into his family portrait. This humble, young woman becomes the mother of the one we all have been waiting for.

"And Mary said, 'Behold, I am the servant of the Lord; let it be to me according to your word.' And the angel departed from her." Luke 1:38

Words of Mary: "My soul magnifies the Lord, and my spirit rejoices in God my Savior, for he has looked on the humble estate of his servant. For behold, from now on all generations will call me blessed." Luke 1:46-48

For more on this story of Mary: Matthew 1:8-25; Luke 1:26-38, 46-55

Mary

Ordinary

December 24th

Joseph was an ordinary carpenter in Nazareth who worked hard with his hands to put food on the table and a roof over his head. He had a good reputation in the town, but it was about to be destroyed. "You want me to take this pregnant woman as my wife?" That's what the angel had said. He knew what people would say about him and Mary. He knew he wasn't the father of this child, but as shocking as it sounded, he believed what the angel said about Mary.

God put Joseph beside Mary, creating a new family. If she was carrying Immanuel, their Rescuer was coming! God would use an ordinary carpenter to protect and care for the greatest treasure humans would ever behold—Jesus. His masterful painting was almost complete.

The angel to Joseph: "Joseph, son of David, do not fear to take Mary as your wife, for that which is conceived in her is from the Holy Spirit. She will bear a son, and you shall call his name Jesus, for he will save his people from their sins...When Joseph woke from sleep, he did as the angel of the Lord commanded him: he took his wife." Matthew 1:20-21, 24

People speaking about Jesus: "Is not this the carpenter's son?" Matthew 13:55a

For more on this story of Joseph: Matthew 1:18-25

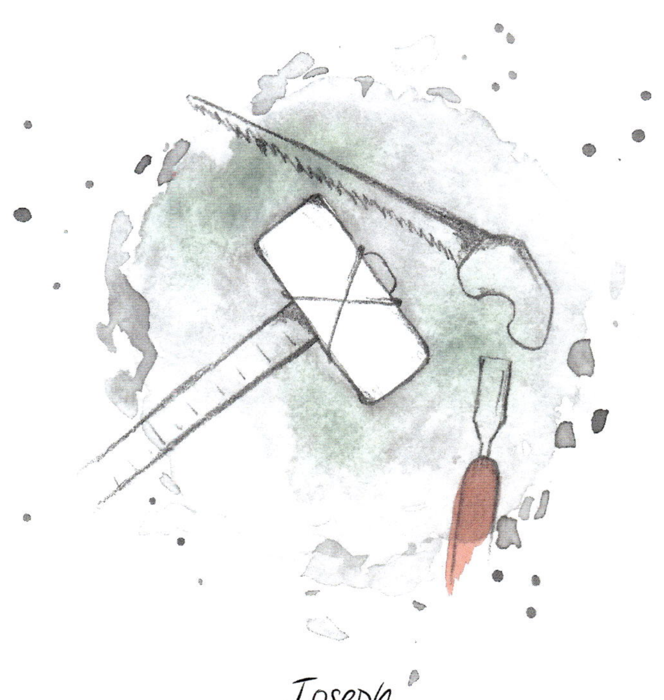

Joseph

Immanuel

December 25th

This moment, this hope, this human is what every beating heart has anticipated. It was time! God's unexpected plan was unfolding right before their eyes in an unassuming village called Bethlehem. Would the Rescuer come with parades and feasts? Crowns and swords flashing? No, this was not God's plan at all. But he definitely came, as God promised, with a great cry of a baby? That's right, Immanuel, the one we've waited for, came as every human does, through the painful labor of a woman. And do you remember what Immanuel means? God with us. Yes, Immanuel was God! And, yes, God painted Himself into this messy family picture. God—A HUMAN, what an astonishing and brilliant plan!

Mary and Joseph named the baby Jesus. This human would live obediently in the good boundaries God made, when every other human would not. He would trust God's plan of rescue when every other human did not. And this broken family he was born into was a masterpiece, telling the world how much God wanted to be with us—unwanted, unloved, disgraced, and disappointing humans.

"And while they were there, the time came for her to give birth. And she gave birth to her firstborn son and wrapped him in swaddling cloths and laid him in a manger, because there was no place for them in the inn."
Luke 2:6-7

Said of Jesus: "...being born in the likeness of men. And being found in human form, he humbled himself by becoming obedient..." Philippians 2:7-8

For more on this story of Jesus: Matthew 1:18-25, Luke 2:1-20, Hebrews 5:7-9, Philippians 2:5-11

Jesus

Today is the biggest birthday celebration of the year, the day Jesus was born into a human family! Today we say, "Thank you for this wonderfully, unexpected plan! We are so glad that you were born and came to be with us on earth!

Happy Birthday, Jesus!

There is so much more to tell about the life of Jesus, so many surprises and questions answered. Wait until you hear about the end of His life! It's not the ending you might expect, because God has no ending—

but that story is for another day.

25 *Days anticipating Jesus' Birthday* Ornaments for your tree

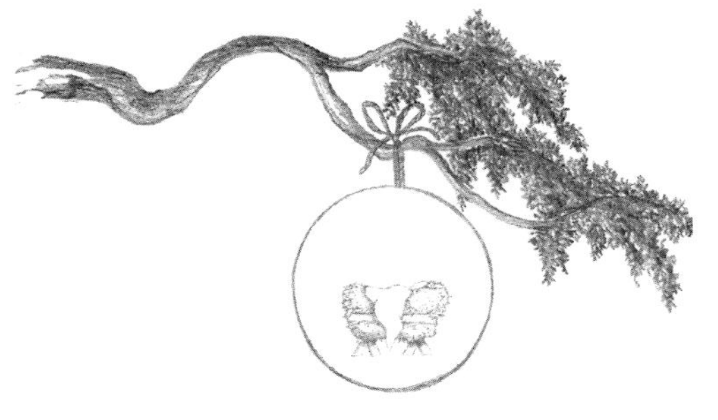

Email kristinkjorlaug@gmail.com and ask for a free PDF of the 25 pencil ornaments (1.5 inch round)

Or you can visit kristinkjorlaug.com for the ornament download link

---

You can also purchase Jesus' Unexpected Family Tree Ornament Coloring Book on Amazon.com (3 inch round ornaments)

Made in the USA
Coppell, TX
22 November 2019